DATE DUE

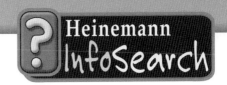

Managing Our Resources

Fossil Fuels
A resource our world depends on

Heinemann Library
Chicago, Illinois

Ian Graham

© 2005 Heinemann Library

a division of Reed Elsevier Inc.

Chicago, Illinois

Customer Service 888-454-2279

Visit our website at
www.heinemannlibrary.com

Designed by David Poole and
Paul Myerscough

Photo research by Melissa Allison and
Andrea Sadler

Originated by Ambassador Litho Ltd.
Printed in China by WKT Company Limited

09 08 07 06

10 9 8 7 6 5 4 3

Library of Congress Cataloging-in-Publication Data
Graham, Ian, 1953-
  Fossil fuels : a resource our world depends on / Ian Graham.
       p. cm. -- (Managing our resources)
  Includes bibliographical references and index.
  ISBN 1-4034-5615-1 (lib. bdg.) --
  ISBN 1-4034-5623-2 (pbk.)
  1. Fossil fuels--Juvenile literature. I. Title.
  TP318.3.G68 2005
  333.8'2--dc22

                          2004005834

Acknowledgments
The author and publisher are grateful to the following for permission to reproduce copyright material: p. 4 top James Field/Simon Girling Associates/Harcourt Education Ltd.; p. 4 bottom Geoff Lane/CSIRO/Science Photo Library; pp. 6, 7, 16, 20 top, 29 PA Photos; pp. 9, 14 17 top, 22, 25 ImageWorks/Topham Picturepoint; p. 10 Hulton-Deutsch Collection/Corbis; p. 11 top NASA; p. 12 Craig Aurness/Corbis; pp. 15 top, 20 bottom, 26 Photodisc/Getty Images; p. 15 bottom left Corbis; p. 15 bottom right BryantMole Books; p. 17 bottom Robert Harding Picture Library; p. 18 Martin Bond/Science Photo Library; p. 19 Pat Groves/Ecoscene; p. 23 Jacques Langevin/Sygma/Corbis; p. 24 AP/Topham Picturepoint; p. 27 Jim Winkley/Ecoscene; p. 28 David Buton/SABA/Corbis.

Cover photograph: Photodisc/Getty Images.

Every effort has been made to contact copyright holders of any material reproduced in this book. Any omissions will be rectified in subsequent printings if notice is given to the publisher.

Contents

Some words are shown in bold, **like this.** You can find out what they mean by looking in the glossary.

What Are Fossil Fuels?

Fossil fuels are natural resources found in the ground. They are coal, oil, and natural gas. They formed from plants and animals that died hundreds of millions of years ago. We release the energy they contain by burning them.

What is coal?

Coal is all that remains of forests that once grew on most of Earth. When the trees died and fell, they were buried under soil and mud. First, they turned into peat, a spongy material that can be dried and burned. As more earth built up on top of the peat, all the water and air were squeezed out and the peat slowly hardened and turned into coal.

Some of the forests that formed the coal we use today were growing even before the dinosaurs walked on Earth.

Millions of years of being pressed together underground changed dead plants into coal.

What is oil?

Oil is a sticky, black liquid formed from the remains of tiny plants and animals, called plankton. They lived in the sea millions of years ago. When they died, they sank to the seabed, where they were covered by mud before they could rot. Over millions of years, heat and the action of **microbes** changed them into oil.

What is natural gas?

Natural gas is a mixture of gases found underground. It is mostly made from a gas called methane. Three other gases— ethane, propane, and butane— are mixed with it. Natural gas usually forms in the same places as oil. It may be dissolved in the oil, like the bubbles in a soft drink. Or it may rise to the top of the oil and become trapped under the rock above it.

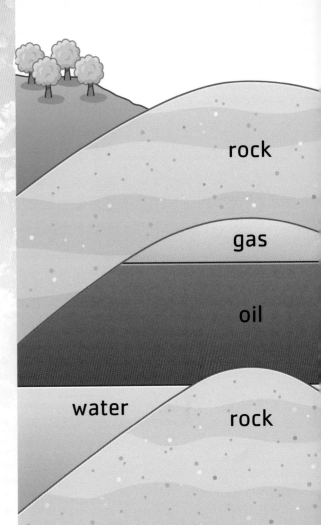

rock

gas

oil

water

rock

Oil and gas become trapped between layers of rock.

Why Are Fossil Fuels Important?

The way we live today depends on using huge amounts of energy for heating, lighting, factories, transportation, and entertainment. Most of this is supplied by fossil fuels. They are used in two main ways. They are burned to produce heat, and they are **processed** to make many different materials. The plastic parts of toys, mobile phones, pens, and many other things we use in our everyday lives are made from fossil fuels. Many of the paints and cleaning products we use in our homes are made from fossil fuels as well.

The effect that using fossil fuels has on environment is also important to know about. The fuels are **extracted** from the ground, processed, and used all over the world. Leaks and spills of fossil fuels and the gases produced when they are burned cause a lot of **pollution**.

Fossil fuels have many uses. In a supermarket, plastic packaging and signs, the floor tiling, and even some of the clothes worn by the staff are made from fossil fuels, mainly oil. The electricity that powers the refrigerators, freezers, and lights comes from fossil fuels, too.

What is the heat from fossil fuels used for?

The heat given off by burning fossil fuels is used in many different ways. It is used to keep buildings warm. It is used in power plants to make electricity. It is also used to make engines and other machines work.

Did you know?

Natural gas was discovered by ancient peoples. The ancient Chinese used natural gas as fuel to boil salty water. They wanted salt, which was left behind after the water had boiled away. The ancient Greeks and Romans used natural gas seeping from the ground to make eternal (never-ending) flames for their **temples** and **shrines**.

Air travel depends on the fossil fuels burned in aircraft engines.

Where Are Fossil Fuels Found?

Fossil fuels are not found everywhere. Coal is found where vast forests grew millions of years ago. Oil and natural gas are found where the ground was once at the bottom of **prehistoric** oceans.

Where are coal and gas found?

Coal is found in more places than oil or natural gas. Some countries that produce a lot of coal include Russia, Ukraine, the United States, and China.

The biggest natural **gas fields** are found in Russia and the Middle East. One of the biggest, the Urengoy field, was found in Russia in the 1960s. The gas is trapped under rock more than 3,280 feet (1,000 meters) below the surface.

Coal is found all over the world.

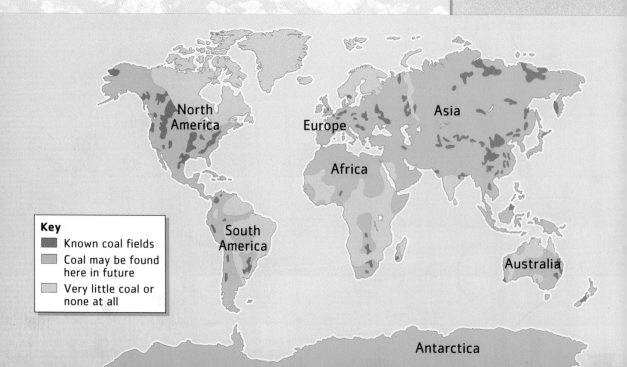

North America

Europe

Asia

Africa

South America

Australia

Key
- Known coal fields
- Coal may be found here in future
- Very little coal or none at all

Antarctica

Where are the biggest oil fields?

The biggest **oil fields** are called supergiants. Only about 40 of the 50,000 oil fields found so far are supergiants. Most of them are in the Middle East, in countries such as Saudi Arabia and Iraq. Saudi Arabia produces more oil than any other country. It contains the world's biggest oil field, called Al-Ghawar. Al-Ghawar is 155 miles (250 kilometers) long and 22 miles (35 kilometers) wide.

The fuel business

The international trade in fossil fuels is one of the world's biggest businesses. Fossil fuels are sold by countries such as the United States and Russia that have a lot of fossil fuels to countries that have little or no fossil fuels, such as France, Belgium, Armenia, and Iceland. Countries with the most fossil fuels, especially countries in the Middle East such as Saudi Arabia and Kuwait, have become very wealthy by selling them.

This is Ras Tanura oil terminal in Saudi Arabia.

How Are Fossil Fuels Found?

Some fossil fuels are found above the ground. The sea sometimes wears down the ground above coal. Pieces of coal break off and the tide washes them onto the seashore. This is called sea coal.

In some places, a thick oily material called **asphalt** forms pools where oil oozes up out of the ground. These pools are also called tar pits and pitch lakes. Some of these pits and lakes have existed for millions of years. One in Los Angeles, California, contains the remains of **prehistoric** animals that became stuck in the thick oil and died. Pitch Lake in Trinidad, which is in the West Indies, contains millions of tons of asphalt. Asphalt collected from Pitch Lake is used to build roads.

Most fossil fuels are buried under the ground, so they have to be found in other ways.

Did you know?

Coal was burned in London, England, for the first time in the year 1228. It was sea coal collected on the seashore in Scotland and northern England. People still collect sea coal today.

How are buried fossil fuels found?

Scientists called geologists find buried fossil fuels by studying rocks on the ground that are found in the same places as fossil fuels. They then look for the same types of rocks to find the fossil fuels. They use photographs of the ground taken from airplanes and **satellites** to find the right rocks.

A satellite in space takes photographs that show a huge area of the ground.

Geologists learn more about rock hidden underground by sending sounds into the ground. The sound waves travel down into the ground and bounce back up from different layers of rock. The longer a sound takes to bounce back, the deeper the rock must be. This is called a **seismic** survey. Finally, people drill into the ground to see if fossil fuels are really there.

Sounds sent down into the ground bounce off the different layers of rocks and give scientists clues about what lies deep underground.

vibrator truck

truck with special vibrator sends sound waves down through the rock

sound waves travel through rock

sensors

paths of seismic waves

sensor truck

truck with sensors picks up returning sound waves

top soil

sand

clay

limestone

sound waves bounce off different types of rock

How Are Fossil Fuels Extracted?

Coal is dug out of the ground. Some coal is so near the surface that it can be reached by scraping away the ground on top of it. This makes a huge hole in the ground, which is called an open-cast, or open-pit, **mine**.

Underground

Usually, coal is much deeper underground. Miners dig down to the coal and use machines to cut it away from rock. As the miners dig down to get to the coal, they construct tunnels to keep the rock above from falling down on top of them.

Coal mining is very dirty and dangerous work. In some mines, big machines can be used to cut out the coal. In others, miners have to drill it out.

Drilling for oil and gas

Oil and gas are reached by drilling down through the ground. Some oil and gas lie underneath the seabed. Drilling platforms, called rigs, stand in the sea. A rig has a tall tower, called a derrick, to hold a drill pipe. An engine spins the pipe so that a sharp drill at the other end cuts through the ground.

As the drill cuts deeper, more lengths of pipe are added at the top to push it down even further. When it reaches oil or gas, they flow up through the drill hole to the surface. Drilling derricks are used in the same way on land.

Did you know?

One of the world's tallest oil rigs stands in the Gulf of Mexico. It is 3,280 feet (1,000 meters) tall. That is more than three times the height of the Eiffel Tower in Paris. Its drill goes 16,000 feet (5,000 meters) down below the seabed. That's greater than the height of Mont Blanc, the highest mountain in Europe!

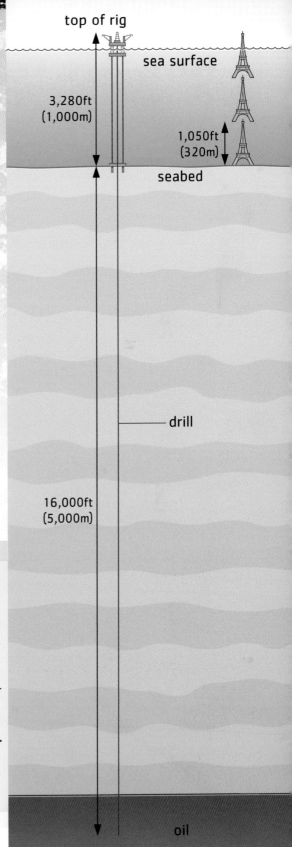

top of rig

sea surface

3,280ft (1,000m)

1,050ft (320m)

seabed

drill

16,000ft (5,000m)

oil

How Are Fossil Fuels Processed?

Fossil fuels are not taken straight out of the ground and used in their natural state. They have to be **processed** to change them into more useful materials.

What is crude oil?

Oil from the ground is also called crude oil, or petroleum. Crude oil is a mixture of a lot of different materials. It is processed in a place called an oil refinery. The refinery's job is to change crude oil into a variety of different liquids and gases that are more useful. The oil is heated and treated with chemicals to split it up.

Oil refineries are huge factories. Oil companies try to use every part of the crude oil so that none is wasted.

What is crude oil made into?

Many things are made from oil. The diesel oil, gas, and kerosene burned in car, ship, and aircraft engines all come from oil. So do the chemicals that are used to make plastics, paints, liquid soaps, and rubber. Some medicines, clothes, and fertilizers are made from chemicals that come from oil. When all of these materials are taken out of crude oil, a sticky, black material called bitumen is left. Even this is useful. Bitumen is used to make roads.

Rubber boots and car tires are not made from natural rubber, which comes from trees. They are made from chemicals that come from oil. Many other objects around us are made from oil, too.

Did you know?

Clarinets and oboes are made from a material called ebonite. This is a very hard type of synthetic, or man-made, rubber. Car tires are made from synthetic rubber, too. And both are made from oil!

How Are Fossil Fuels Moved Around?

Coal, oil, and natural gas have to be moved from where they are found to where they are **processed** and from there to where they are used. They are transported in a number of different ways.

How is coal transported?

Coal is carried away from the **coal face** on a **conveyor belt** and then lifted to the surface. From there, it is transported by freight train, ship, and truck. At power plants, coal is sometimes brought inside through a pipeline. To make it flow through the pipe, the coal is first mixed with water. Inside the power plants, the water drains away and the coal is burned.

The biggest oil tankers c each carry more than 100,000 tons of oil.

How are oil and gas moved?

Oil is transported by pipelines and **tankers**. The biggest oil tanker ships are called supertankers. Some of them are more than 1,300 feet (400 meters) long.

That is the same as four soccer fields lying end to end.

Natural gas is transported by pipelines, special gas carrier ships, and tankers trucks. Nearly all of the natural gas used today is moved by pipeline, flowing through the pipes as a gas. To transport natural gas on ships, it is cooled down to below −258.7 °F (−161.5 °C) so that it changes to a liquid, called liquid natural gas, or LNG. When the ships arrive at their destination, the liquid is changed back to a gas by carefully warming it up.

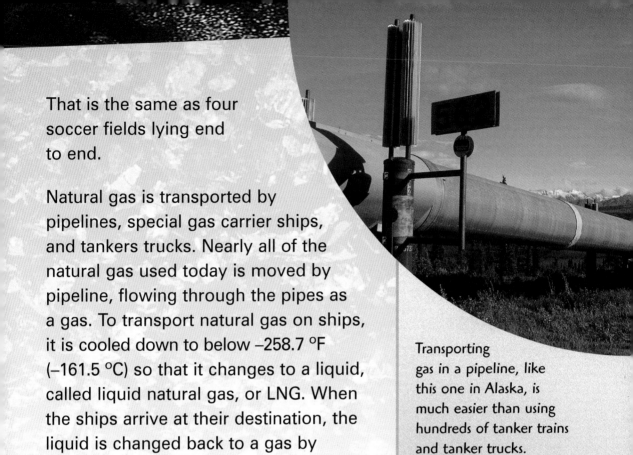

Transporting gas in a pipeline, like this one in Alaska, is much easier than using hundreds of tanker trains and tanker trucks.

Once fossil fuels have been moved, they need to be stored. Coal can be piled up on the ground. Oil and gas are stored in tanks, like the gas tanks shown here.

How Do Power Plants Use Fossil Fuels?

Power plants are giant machines designed to produce electricity. They need energy to do it. Most power plants get the energy they need from coal, oil, or natural gas.

A power plant looks very complicated, but it carries out a series of the following very simple steps:

1. Coal, oil, or natural gas is burned to produce heat.

2. The heat boils water in a tank, called a **boiler,** to make steam.

3. The steam blows through a machine called a **turbine** and makes it spin.

4. The spinning turbine drives a machine called a generator that actually makes the electricity.

Coal-fired power plants need a constant supply of coal, delivered by the trainload every day.

Did you know?

Energy cannot be made or destroyed. It can only be changed from one form into another. A power plant changes the energy stored in its fuel into another form of energy—electricity.

CASE STUDY:
Drax Power Plant

The Drax power plant near Selby in the United Kingdom is one of the world's biggest power plants. Everything about the Drax power plant is huge. Each of its six **boilers** is as tall as a fifteen-story building. They burn about 38,000 tons of coal every day. The coal is crushed to a fine powder so that it burns quickly.

How much electricity does Drax produce?

Drax supplies one tenth of Great Britain's electricity . The amount of electricity produced by a big power plant like Drax is measured in gigawatt-hours. One gigawatt-hour is an enormous amount of energy. It is enough to keep 700,000 lightbulbs lit for a entire day and night. Drax produces about 24,000 gigawatt-hours of electricity every year.

Steam rises from the cooling towers of Drax power plant.

How Can Extracting Fossil Fuels Be Dangerous?

Extracting fossil fuels from the ground is dangerous. **Mines** can collapse or flood with water. They can fill up with natural gas. There may be harmful dust in the air. Coal, oil, and natural gas catch fire easily, so fire is a danger, too.

Why is dust in coal mines harmful?

Dust in coal mines is not the same as dust in your home. It contains tiny, sharp pieces of rock. If they are breathed in year after year, they can damage people's lungs and make it more difficult to breathe. Spraying water and blowing air through a mine helps to keep dust down.

Mining for coal is a very dirty and dangerous job.

Did you know?

Coal miners used to take birds underground with them. Poisonous gas in the mine would quickly affect the birds and warn the miners, giving them more time to escape.

Why are there harmful gases in coal mines?

As dead plants change into coal, gases are produced. When miners cut into the coal, any gas still there may escape into the mine. Most of it is a gas called methane. If this gas mixes with air, a spark can make it explode.

A poisonous gas called carbon monoxide is sometimes produced, too. It can suffocate people. If another poisonous gas, called **hydrogen** sulphide, leaks into a mine, everyone knows about it right away because it smells like rotten eggs!

The dangers of drilling

Drilling for gas is very dangerous. The gas must not be allowed to escape because it catches fire very easily. Several gas platforms, which drill for gas under the sea, have been destroyed when leaking gas caught fire.

The Piper Alpha offshore oil rig in the North Sea was destroyed by a gas explosion and fire on July 6, 1988. 167 people died in the accident.

How Can Using Fossil Fuels Harm the Environment?

Extracting and using fossil fuels causes **pollution.** Open-cast mining produces big, ugly holes in the land. **Mines,** oil wells, and gas wells can produce a lot of heavy traffic in places of great natural beauty.

Burning fossil fuels produces air pollution, which makes buildings dirty and affects people's health. Breathing in the smoke and **fumes** produced when fossil fuels are burned can make breathing disorders, such as asthma and bronchitis, worse. The smoke produced by burning fossil fuels, especially coal and oil, contains substances that can cause serious diseases if they are breathed in for a long time.

Heavy traffic produces so much smoke and fumes that the air in modern cities is often badly polluted.

How can fossil fuels harm the sea?

Accidents involving oil **tankers** and drilling rigs pollute the sea. Oil leaking from an oil tanker or an offshore oil well floats on top of the water. Seabirds that land in the oil become coated with it. They clean their feathers with their beaks and swallow so much oil that they often die. In time, the action of sunlight and the weather changes the oil and it sinks. When it reaches the seabed, it can kill the plants and sea creatures that live there. Close to the shore, it can kill or pollute shellfish. Oil washed up along a coast can cover the seashore with a black, sticky, smelly layer.

The air over large parts of Kuwait turned into a choking black fog during the Gulf War in 1991 because of oil wells that were burning.

Did you know?

Burning fossil fuels produces gases called greenhouse gases that soak up heat from the Sun and warm Earth. This is slowly changing the world's climate and weather and could produce more storms, floods, and **droughts**.

CASE STUDY:
The Exxon Valdez Oil Spill

On March 24, 1989, the *Exxon Valdez* oil **tanker** strayed into shallow water in Prince William Sound, Alaska. Rocks just under the surface ripped through the ship. About 39,000 tons of oil poured out—enough to fill 125 swimming pools. Winds and waves carried the oil to shore.

How did the oil affect wildlife?

About 10,000 people went to the region immediately after the spill to try to save wildlife. People sprayed the oil with chemicals to break it down and shoveled it up. Even so, about 250,000 birds, 2,800 sea otters, 300 seals, and 22 whales are thought to have died. Billions of fish eggs were probably destroyed as well. Wildlife takes a long time to recover from a disaster of this size. The numbers of some seabirds, seals, sea otters, and shellfish had still not recovered more than ten years after the disaster.

The *Exxon Valdez* oil spill in Alaska killed hundreds of thousands of creatures.

Will Fossil Fuels Ever Run Out?

Every year the world uses fossil fuels that took more than one million years to form. New fossil fuels are being made, but not quickly enough to keep up with our demand for them. One day they will run out.

How long will fossil fuels last?

Many scientists agree that all the **oil fields** we know about today will have run dry in about 40 years. **Gas fields** will last about 65 years. Oil and gas will actually last longer than this because new fields are still being found. Even so, a time will come when no new oil and gas fields will be found and the old fields will run out.

Coal will last far longer than oil or gas. The **coal fields** we know about today will last at least another 200 years.

We are using up the world's oil in our cars, trucks, and power plants so fast that it will run out in the near future.

How Can We Conserve Fossil Fuels?

Although fossil fuels will eventually run out, we could make them last longer by using them more slowly. Turning off the lights when you leave a room and turning the heating in your home down a few degrees would save a tiny amount of energy every day. If millions of people did the same thing, all the small savings would add up to a big saving in fossil fuels. Walking or riding a bike sometimes, instead of going everywhere by car, would save more fossil fuels. **Recycling** plastic things would help to reduce the amount of new plastic that has to be made from oil.

The family in this house has left out plastic and other waste ready to be collected for recycling.

We could burn less gas and oil in vehicles. We could build houses that hold more heat inside, so less fuel has to be burned to keep them warm. We could make electricity in different ways, without burning coal, oil, or gas. There are many options open to us.

How is electricity made without fossil fuels?

The wind, waves, tides, rivers, sunlight, and even heat from deep underground can supply energy to make electricity. Unlike fossil fuels, these sources of energy will not run out. That is why this type of energy is called renewable energy.

Some electricity is already being made from renewable sources—mainly wind and water. However, developing other sources of energy is very expensive. It is difficult to develop renewable energy sources that are no more expensive than electricity produced from fossil fuels.

How can we use less gas and oil?

We could make fewer car trips by using buses and trains. Of course, most buses and trains use fossil fuels, too. But one full bus can replace dozens of car trips, and one train can replace hundreds of car trips. We could also drive cars with smaller engines that burn less fuel, or with engines that use different fuels.

Wind **turbines** like these in Denmark make electricity from the wind.

What kind of cars do not burn gas or oil?

Electric cars are powered by electric motors instead of engines. Although they do not burn gas or oil, the electricity that charges their batteries comes from power plants. And that electricity is often created by burning fossil fuels.

A new type of electric car, powered by a **fuel cell** instead of a battery, is being designed. A fuel cell makes electricity by combining **hydrogen** and oxygen.

There are also cars that use electric motors as well as gas engines. These are known as hybrid cars. They use much less gasoline than cars that only have gas engines.

Electric cars run on battery power instead of burning gas or oil.

CASE STUDY:
A Fuel Cell Car

The Mercedes-Benz *F-Cell* car is a **prototype** car powered by a **fuel cell**. It can reach a speed of 62 miles (100 kilometers) an hour in 16 seconds and has a top speed of about 85 miles (140 kilometers) an hour. It can be driven a distance of about 185 miles (300 kilometers) on a full tank of **hydrogen**.

Why are there so few fuel cell cars?

Fuel cell cars are so new that they are still being tested. They are not yet ready to be sold to the public. Before they can go on sale, gas stations will have to be fitted with new pumps so that fuel cell cars can be refueled as easily as any car today.

The Mercedes *F-Cell* looks like a normal car, but it is powered by a fuel cell instead of gas.

Glossary

asphalt thick, black or dark brown liquid made from oil. Natural asphalt is found in small pools or larger lakes where oil has oozed out of the ground.

boiler tank where water is boiled to produce hot water or steam

coal face part of a coal mine where miners cut the coal away from the surrounding rock

coal field place under the ground where there is a large amount of coal

conveyor belt loop of material driven by rollers and used to carry materials short distances

drought long period of time when there is no rain, leaving the ground too dry to grow plants

extract take something out of something else, such as coal out of a field

fuel cell device that makes electricity from the chemical reaction between hydrogen and oxygen gases

fume harmful or unpleasant gas, smoke, or vapor

gas field place under the ground where there is a large amount of natural gas

hydrogen chemical element that is found in nature as a flammable, colorless, and odorless gas

microbe tiny living organism that can only be seen by using a microscope

mining digging into the ground to reach valuable materials, such as coal

oil field place under the ground where there is a large amount of oil

pollution harmful or poisonous substances in nature, usually produced by the activities of humans

prehistoric time before people started writing

process to change a material by using a series of actions or treatments

prototype first example of a car, plane, or any other product built to test things and make sure that the product works properly

recycle to process for reuse instead of using materials only once and then throwing them away

satellite small object that orbits around a larger object, such as a spacecraft going around Earth

seismic caused by an earthquake or vibration of Earth caused by something else, such as an explosion

shrine place that is considered sacred

tanker vehicle or ship designed to carry a large amount of liquid

temple building in which people worship

turbine engine with winglike parts that are spun around by the pressure of water, steam, or gas

More Books to Read

Alcraft, Rob. *Oil Disasters.* Chicago: Heinemann Library, 1999.

Bryan, Nichol. *Exxon Valdez: Oil Spill.* Milwaukee, Wis.: Gareth Stevens, 2003.

Edwards, Ron, and Adrianna Edwards. *Oil and Gas.* New York: Crabtree Publishing, 2004.

Graham, Ian. *Fossil Fuels: A Resource Our World Depends On.* Chicago: Heinemann Library, 2004.

Greeley, August. *Sludge and Slime: Oil Spills in Our World.* New York: Rosen Publishing, 2003.

Miller, Kimberly M. *What If We Run Out of Fossil Fuels?* Danbury, Conn.: Scholastic Library, 2002.

Sherman, Josepha. *Fossil Fuel Power.* Bloomington, Minn.: Capstone Press, 2004.

Snedden, Robert. *Energy from Fossil Fuels.* Chicago: Heinemann Library, 2001.

Index